D1121439

HOT TOPICS

GLOBAL ECONOMY

Richard Spilsbury

Chicago, Illinois

www.capstonepub.com
Visit our website to find out more information about Heinemann-Raintree books.

To order:
Phone 888-454-2279
Visit www.capstonepub.com to browse our catalog and order online.

an imprint of Capstone Global Library, LLC
Chicago, Illinois

Visit our website at www.heinemannraintree.com

Edited by Adam Miller, Nick Hunter, and Diyan Leake
Designed by Philippa Jenkins
Original illustrations © Capstone Global Library Ltd 2012
Picture research by Mica Brancic
Production by Eirian Griffiths and Alison Parsons
Originated by Capstone Global Library Ltd
Printed and bound in the USA by Corporate Graphics

15 14 13 12 11
10 9 8 7 6 5 4 3 2 1

Library of Congress Cataloging-in-Publication Data
Spilsbury, Richard, 1963-
Global economy / Richard Spilsbury.
p. cm.—(Hot topics)
Includes bibliographical references and index.
ISBN 978-1-4329-6038-4 (hb)—ISBN 978-1-4329-6046-9 (pb) 1. International economic relations—Juvenile literature. 2. International trade—Juvenile literature. 3. International finance—Juvenile literature. 4. Globalization—Economic aspects—Juvenile literature. I. Title.
HF1359.S696 2012
337—dc23 2011017910

Acknowledgments
The author and publisher are grateful to the following for permission to reproduce copyright material: Corbis pp. 5 (epa/© Raminder Pal Singh), 11 (© Scott McDermott), 17 (Reuters/© Jitendra Prakash), 20 (epa/© Arshad Arbab), 21 (Visions of America/© Joseph Sohm), 24 (© Robert Wallis), 29 (Reuters/© Andrew Winning), 31 (Zuma Press/© Aristidis Vafeiadakis), 33 (epa/© Tian Di), 34 (Sygma/© Sophie Elbaz), 36 (epa/© Tian Weitao), 37 (Reuters/© Sukree Sukplang), 38 (VII/© John Stanmeyer), 42 (epa/© Everett Kennedy Brown), 45 (Sygma/© John Van Hasselt), 49 (epa/© Divyakant Solanki), 50 (Reuters/© Osman Orsal), 52 (Reuters/© Nir Elias), 55 (© Ashley Cooper); Getty Images pp. 18 (AFP Photo/Ronaldo Schemidt), 26 (Christopher Furlong); © Simon Rawles p. 46; Shutterstock pp. 10 (© Abutyrin), 12 (© Faraways), 40 (© Romanenkova), 58 (© Smith&Smith).

Cover photograph reproduced with permission of Shutterstock (© Andrea Danti).

Every effort has been made to contact copyright holders of material reproduced in this book. Any omissions will be rectified in subsequent printings if notice is given to the publishers.

CONTENTS

Some words are printed in bold, **like this**. You can find out what they mean by looking in the glossary.

WHAT IS THE GLOBAL ECONOMY?

In 2008–2009, the world's economy was in crisis. Banks, and even countries, stood on the brink of **bankruptcy**. But what is an economy? What makes it global, and how does it make a difference to people's lives?

Economy

The economy is all about buying and selling and keeping track of money. It describes how **resources**—including land, workers, and raw materials—and money are managed to produce and sell some **goods** and **services** and then buy others. Goods include products such as cell phones, carpeting, and chocolate. Services are duties or tasks done for others that people are paid for, such as teaching or driving a bus.

Economies happen on many different scales. A simple local economy might include a dairy farmer, a dairy factory that bottles milk, a local market, and a customer. A regional economy might include many different sorts of farmers and all the products they grow or farm, factories to process the products, a large number of customers, and people who deal with waste generated through production and use. You can imagine how complex international economies are. The global economy is the trade and production relationship between countries around the world.

Economy is "the state of a country or area in terms of the production and consumption of goods and services and the supply of money"

***Concise Oxford Dictionary*, 11th edition, 2004**

■ Cell phones are an example not only of a product of the global economy, but also a globally used technology. In India alone there are around 800 million cell phone users.

A typical cell phone is a product of the global economy. The cell phone company may be based in Europe or Japan, with offices worldwide responsible for design and marketing. The phone is made from natural resources, including oil used for the plastic parts and the mineral coltan. Coltan is found in the Congo and is used in electronic parts to control electricity flow. Many individual parts, such as screens and processors, are made in China, but cell phones may be constructed in factories based in other countries, such as Hungary or Romania. The cell phones are sold worldwide in stores and online, often via different regional cell phone network providers, from Claro in Argentina to Telstra in Australia.

The start of the global economy

The global economy connects the individual economies of every country around the world. Countries have been linked ever since traders started crossing borders and seas, especially in the age of empires. For example, the ancient Egyptians used spices from southeast Asia, which they bought from seafaring Arabs to mummify their pharaohs. During ancient Roman times, there was widespread trade in many goods such as glassware, olive oil, and metals from all around the Roman Empire.

However, many historians recognize that the global economy had its beginnings in the late 15th century, when European countries started a series of voyages of discovery. These included Christopher Columbus's 1492 voyage to the Americas, on behalf of Spain, and Portuguese Vasco da Gama's 1497 voyage to India. The motives for these voyages were to find resources to sell at a profit in Europe, including spices, and to spread influence and religion around the world. The voyages were made possible by technology which included ships capable of sailing long distances. They were often funded by **loans** of money from some of the first banks ever established.

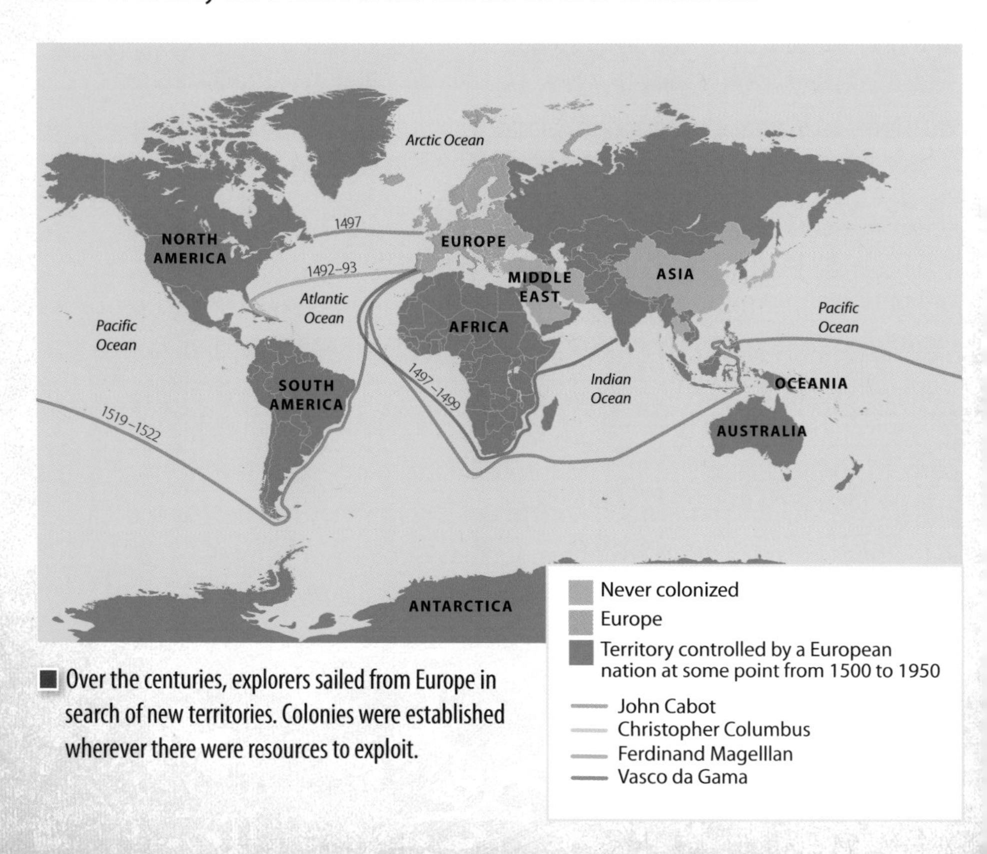

Over the centuries, explorers sailed from Europe in search of new territories. Colonies were established wherever there were resources to exploit.

Between 1500 and 1800, European countries established and controlled colonies around the word. These supplied resources and goods for their economies. For example, in the Americas, Spanish and Portuguese colonies were set up in the **Caribbean**, near where Columbus landed. Other colonies were established in South America, in areas where sugar grew and near gold and silver mines. Later, British and French colonies established tobacco, cotton, and other **plantations** in North America. The colonies were a source of raw materials and goods for the empire, and served also as a market for the manufactured goods made in the home country. Both activities made the home country's economy larger.

The colonists forced slaves, who were mostly from other countries, to work on their plantations or in their mines to produce goods. Ships took the goods back to Europe, and the empty ships filled up with more slaves in Africa, which were traded for goods such as textiles and iron. The slaves were then transported to the Americas. Slaves were often kept and transported in appalling conditions, and hundreds of thousands died during this slave trade.

The 19th century

In the late 18th to 19th centuries, the **Industrial Revolution** in Europe and America brought about another leap forward in global economic growth. Steam-driven and, later, fuel-driven engines were invented that could power large machines to increase production. Coal and other fossil fuel industries expanded to supply power for the machines.

A new network of railroads, canals, and ocean transport systems ensured that raw materials and goods could be moved in bulk around the world. The Industrial Revolution not only used new power sources, but it also involved moving production out of homes and cottages and into large factories.

WHAT DO YOU THINK?

Wealth generated by slavery was important for funding economic growth in both the United States and the United Kingdom. For example, in 1840, sales of cotton produced by slaves in the United States made up over half of the country's **export** earnings. Seventy percent of cotton used in British textile mills, and sold from cities such as Manchester, came from the United States.

Is modern slave labor still helping economic growth today?

The global economy since World War II

Two damaging and costly world wars slowed the growth of the global economy in the first half of the 20th century, but it then picked up again. There was rapid reconstruction and development of industries and **infrastructure** in nations damaged by the war. The United States, with no damage to buildings or infrastructure during the war, became the world's largest economy, through lending money for reconstruction and partly through selling technologies the world wanted, such as televisions and faster airplanes. This was helped by many things, such as falling fuel and transportation costs. The total value of world **export** trade rose from $58 billion in 1950 to $5.3 trillion in 1997.

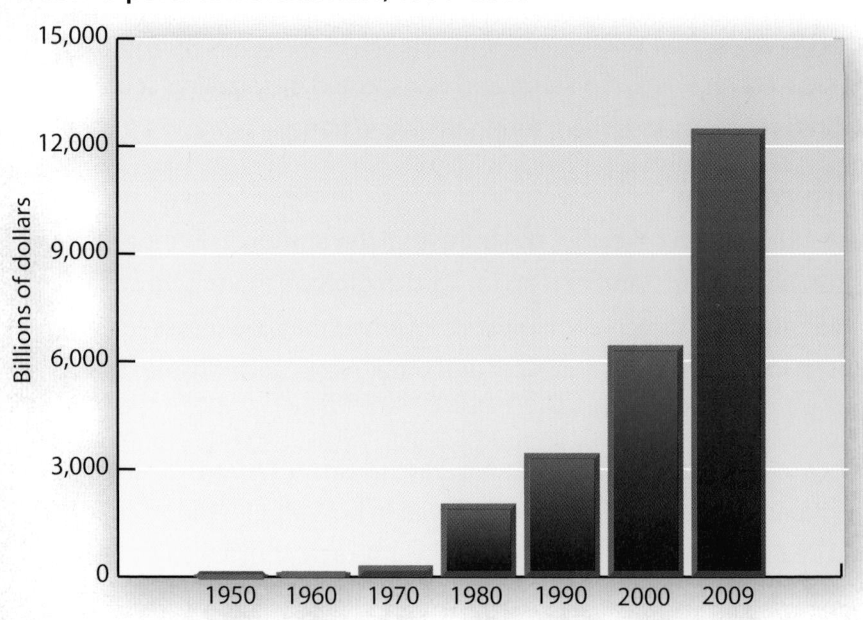

This chart shows that global exports are more than 40 times greater than they were about 60 years ago.

From the 1960s to the 1980s, advances in technology and manufacturing techniques spread, allowing Asian economies such as Japan to expand. These developments also helped Germany to become the largest European economy. From the 1990s onward, countries such as India, China, and Brazil, all rich in natural resources and with enormous populations to provide low-cost labor, have emerged with a greater share of the global economy.

Economic growth

The value of a nation's output of services and goods in a given year is called its **gross domestic product (GDP).** GDP measures the value in money of services and goods produced using the nation's resources (for more information, see page 56). If we take the effects of inflation out of GDP, then we have real GDP. To judge how valuable a country is in economic terms, people compare how real GDP changes over time. This is known as its economic growth. The following table illustrates the economic growth of different countries.

The Chinese economy grew because its factories were producing more goods for global sale. Economies can also grow when a country finds and exploits valuable new natural resources such as oil. The U.S. and Japanese economies shrank partly because important industries struggled when cheaper goods were made in other countries such as China. When there is more than a few months of shrinking economy, a nation officially has a **recession**. Many countries went into recession during the global economic crisis of 2008 to 2010 (see pages 28–31). When unemployment rises and spending falls over a longer period, a recession turns into a **depression**.

Percentage change in real GDP

	2007	2008	2009	2010	2011
United States	1.9	0.0	-2.6	2.6	2.2
Japan	2.4	-1.2	-5.2	2.7	1.1
China	13.0	9.6	9.1	10.1	8.9
European Union	2.9	0.5	-4.2	1.8	1.6

GREAT DEPRESSION

The longest and worst depression in modern times happened from 1929 to 1939. It started in the United States when the value of businesses suddenly fell, causing people to withdraw their money from banks. Many banks closed. There were fewer banks to provide loans to industry, production fell by a third, and more than a quarter of Americans became unemployed. The Great Depression spread worldwide because U.S. loans were important to other economies. World trade halved and there was political turmoil, allowing the rise of Hitler in Germany and bringing about World War II.

PARTS OF THE GLOBAL ECONOMY

Any economy, global or otherwise, has three main parts: production, trade, and money supply. All are interrelated as money is needed to produce things and trade is needed to make money.

Production

The word *production*, in terms of economics, is the process of turning inputs into outputs. It covers everything that has a value and can be sold. Some of the main categories of goods include raw materials, such as diamonds or water, land, farmed goods, and manufactured goods. Most goods cannot be sold without services including transportation, advertising, and storage. Some services are vital for society, such as healthcare, education, and waste management. Others, such as theme parks, are for entertainment.

This open-pit coal mine produces fuel for use in power plants.

CASE STUDY

Hair for sale

Human hair is in demand for making hair extensions and wigs in many rich countries. Women can sell their hair to make money when there are few other opportunities to work. Black hair, usually from China and India, is plentiful but blonde hair, which is most common in northern Europe and Russia, is more valuable as it is scarcer and also can be dyed to match any color of hair.

In Mossalsk, Russia, the agricultural industry collapsed in the 1990s. A hair-processing corporation called Belli Capelli is one of the few thriving businesses, selling both to rich Moscow salons and to those in Germany and the United States. Workers there collect and clean hair, before packing it for export. In 2011, local women could sell their braided hair over 15 inches (40 centimeters) long to the corporation for almost $50. Sales in Mossalsk rise at the start of school or college terms because students sell their hair for money to buy new books!

Long, blonde hair can be made into extensions for use in fashion shows.

Supply and demand

Economists often talk about economies in terms of **supply** and **demand**. Supply is making goods or services that people need or want. Demand is the desire or need for goods or services that people want to buy or use. The two are closely related. In theory, when there is greater demand, then goods or services cost more, and when demand drops, so do prices. But this depends on what is being sold. For example, rice, bread, and pasta are essential staple foods, forming the main part of the diets of many people in the world. Demand generally remains high whatever the price.

World trade

Trade includes exports, when what is produced is sold to other countries, and **imports**, when goods and services are brought in from other countries. Each country trades what it can produce best because then it can compete more successfully for sales with other countries. For example, the exports that bring in between 40 and 50 percent of Germany's GDP are mainly of machinery, vehicles, chemicals, metals, manufactured goods, foods, and textiles. Germany's trade is usually described as **capital-intensive**. This means that its goods and services are competitive because they are produced by a skilled and educated workforce using advanced technology and machinery. Ethiopia is an example of a **land-intensive** trading nation because its economy is based on agriculture and, therefore, on its soil.

Trade without restrictions

Countries may export and import goods and services freely with each other. This sort of trade without any restrictions is called **free trade**. The idea is that imports offer more choice for consumers, force businesses within that country to produce better goods and services at better prices, and supply important raw materials and other useful products that businesses need. Free trade should also promote cooperation between countries and the exchange of knowledge.

Metal containers are basic units of world trade that can be loaded with various goods and transported globally by ship, road, rail, or air.

Many countries put up barriers to imports to prevent free trade. This is called **protectionism** and it is often used to protect industries from competition. For example, a country might limit how many pairs of cheaper shoes are imported so that its own shoe industry can sell the shoes it makes.This type of protectionism is called an import **quota**. Countries can also protect industries using payments called **subsidies**. For example, a country might subsidize its car industry so it can make cheaper cars than the equivalent imported cars.

Protectionism is sometimes the result of disagreements between countries due to the way a country's people are treated or due to political reasons. For example, the United States banned imports from North Korea in 2008 mainly because it was illegally developing nuclear weapons.

CASE STUDY

Recognizing sardines

Do you ever eat sardines in a can? The sardine fishing industry is an example of how protectionism can harm a less-developed country. There is not just one species of sardine; there are several similar ones. In 2001, the **European Union (EU)** made a law saying that only the species caught in European waters could be sold as sardines. This meant that sardines caught in the waters off Peru could not be sold in Europe as sardines, but instead had to be labeled as different kinds of fish—pilchards or sprats.

Sardines are much more popular in Europe than are pilchards or sprats. And the sardine industry is important to the Peruvian economy and provides a livelihood for many poor fishermen. Therefore, the Peru fishing industry took the European Union to court to fight the decision and, by 2002, the law had been found to be unfair by the **World Trade Organization (WTO)**. Since then, Peru has had an equal opportunity to sell its sardines on European store shelves.

Money supply

The global economy relies on a supply of money to pay for production and trading. Money supply is taken care of by banks and other parts of the financial industry. Say you have a part-time job and want to save for a new bicycle. You might save your money in a bank. The bank gives you small amounts of money called **interest** in return for them keeping your money safe. But banks are businesses, so why would they do that?

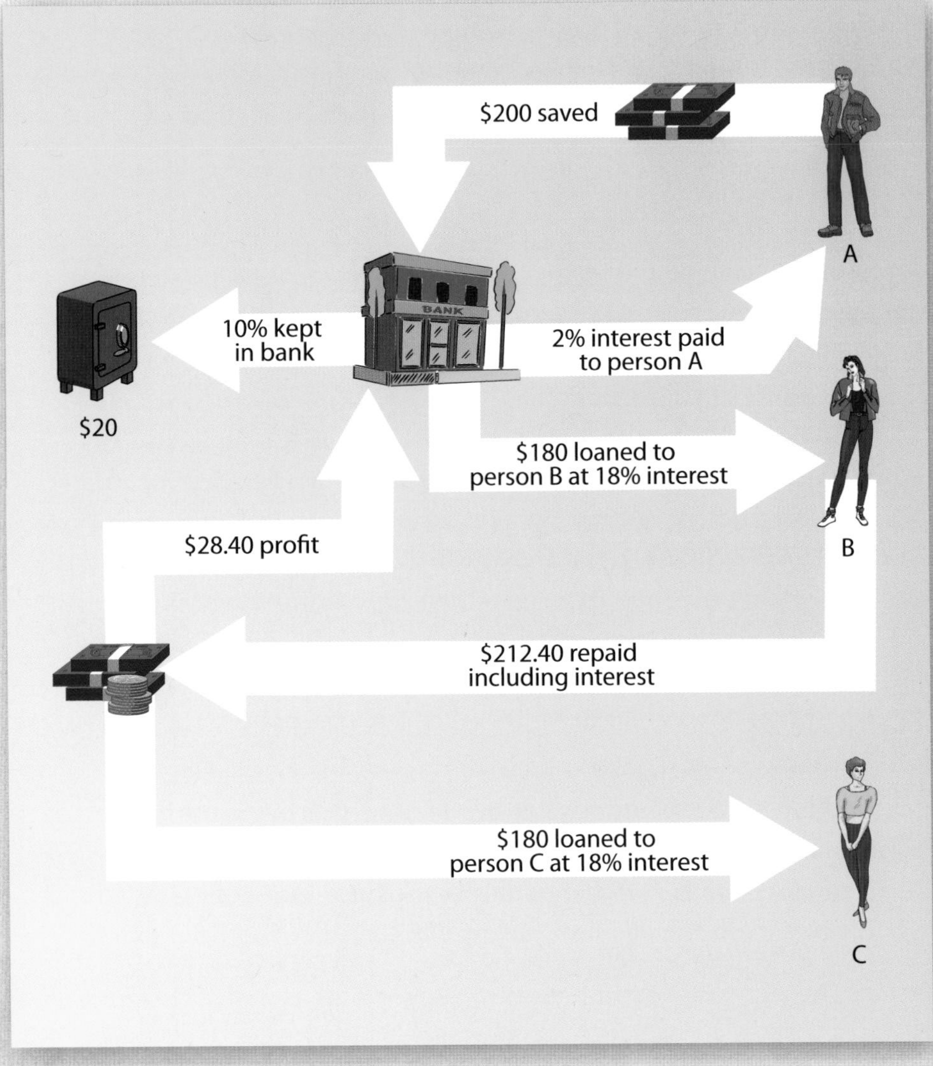

This diagram shows how banks make a profit by charging interest on the loans that customers take out.

BONDS: SPECIAL LOANS

Large organizations, from businesses to governments, sometimes need to find large amounts of money—for example, to buy other businesses or to build new highways. They cannot always borrow large amounts from banks so they issue bonds. Bonds are a little bit like IOUs. When investors pay for bonds in a government, they are basically lending money to the government. Over time, the government pays back the loan, with interest at an agreed amount. The interest is lower when compared to buying **shares** of stock, but bonds are less risky because repayments are independent of the rise and fall in share prices.

Banks also sell money in the form of loans and other financial products such as mortgages. Loans are when people borrow money, usually to pay for something expensive, such as a car. Mortgages are special long-term loans for buying houses and other properties. People who take out loans have to gradually pay back the amount they borrowed, plus interest. Banks make money because the interest they charge on loans is higher than the interest they pay out on savings. Banks also make money in other ways. For example, they charge money for **foreign exchange** for those businesses, in one country, that need to to pay businesses in other countries that use a different currency.

Stock markets

Every business has a value based on how much money it cost to set up, how much it earns, and how much it costs to run, such as wages for workers. Say a business invents a new product and wants to set up a new factory in which to make it. In order to raise money, the owner can sell shares in the business to others. Each share represents part ownership in the business. People owning shares receive payments based on how much the business earns.

The share price in any business changes all the time, depending on many factors. These include whether the business expands as well as government changes, such as the taxes it makes businesses pay, and global changes in the price of fuel for transportation. Investors make money buying shares at low prices and selling them to others when they are worth more. A **stock market** is a place where people trade in many different companies' shares. There are many stock markets worldwide, including the New York Stock Exchange.

WHO CONTROLS THE GLOBAL ECONOMY?

The global economy involves billions of people worldwide and is controlled by governments, big corporations, and global organizations. To make profits and to influence global development, these groups control who trades with whom, how much money is loaned, and where production happens.

Global institutions

There are several global institutions that regulate trade and global development. The World Trade Organization (WTO), originally known as the General Agreement of Tariffs and Trade, was set up in 1995 to supervise free trade. It represents 153 member nations. The WTO resolves trade disputes between countries (see case study on page 23) by assisting in trade negotiations. Decisions made by the WTO are based on what the majority of members agree on. However, the most powerful trading nations, such as the United States, China, and India, have great influence on other nations because countries with smaller economies want to do business with them.

The **International Monetary Fund (IMF)** specializes in helping financial cooperation between countries, such as agreements on exchange rates for different currencies among central banks. It also makes loans to countries with financial difficulties, especially if they are importing a greater value of goods and services than they are exporting. The closely related **World Bank** is an institution that lends money to countries for development. The World Bank's reserves are paid by member countries, and those that pay in more have more say over development projects.

The River Ganges has great social and religious importance in India. Between 2009 and 2014, the World Bank will have loaned $1 billion to India for cleaning it up.

Problems with institutions

The work of the IMF and the World Bank is controversial. Their purpose is to make loans to encourage free trade. For example, the IMF might loan money to mining and other industries that can produce goods for export. However, they may insist on conditions, such as making a country remove food or fuel subsidies, so that other countries' imports have a better chance of selling. The conditions may also include reducing state control of industries, such as water or power supply, so that private, often foreign, companies can invest. Some people argue that such conditions can make countries too economically dependent on others. Furthermore, the interest on loan repayments can be so high that countries struggle to repay their debt and have some money left to develop their countries.

WHAT DO YOU THINK?

In 2010, Ireland was in recession because Irish banks were struggling to repay loans. The country asked for a loan of billions of euros from the IMF and European Union. The conditions of the loan included higher taxes, a lower minimum wage, and loss of **public sector** jobs. Is it fair that ordinary Irish taxpayers should pay for economic problems caused by the banking industry?

Governments

Governments want their industries to succeed in the global economy so that their countries get richer. In the case of democratic governments, this is because they might not be elected again if industries fail. One of the simplest ways they can help international trade is to establish informal links with other countries to promote free trade, so that each can increase the other's exports. For example, in November 2010, British Prime Minister David Cameron led a trade delegation to India. He said that he wanted to make the United Kingdom the "partner of choice" for India. This would ensure there would be jobs for the United Kingdom. In return, the British government announced that it would allow the export of British civil nuclear technology to India for the first time.

Governments can also set up formal trading blocs to assist trade. These are groupings of countries with closely linked economies, usually for political or geographical reasons. Most of the 27 countries of the European Union use the same currency—the euro. The European Union is the world's largest trading bloc. It has greater global economic power than any of its member countries, for example, in establishing world free-trade laws or aiding foreign investment in industries in its countries. The North American Free Trade Association (NAFTA), is another trading bloc. It works to remove barriers to trade between the United States and its close neighbors, Canada and Mexico. There are similar groupings in regions all around the world.

Trade leaders from Canada, Mexico, and the United States met at a NAFTA meeting in 2011.

CASE STUDY

Asian Tigers

In the 1960s, the governments of Taiwan, Hong Kong, South Korea, and Singapore worked together to improve their economies. They decided to attract investment from highly industrialized countries, including the United Kingdom, to expand their industries, notably manufacturing goods ranging from electrical equipment and clothing to cars. This was beneficial to the foreign countries, as East Asia could supply cheaper goods. With the outside investment, these Asian countries improved education, training, and research into new products, which created an even more efficient workforce.

Exports soon exceeded imports, as they were relatively small countries with low import requirements, and the countries got richer. Economic growth averaged 6 percent for nearly 30 years, and the average Korean's wealth grew by six times. The countries were known as Asian Tigers because their economic performance relative to other countries was so powerful and ferocious.

At the end of the 1990s, the Tigers' fortunes changed. Financial institutions increasingly gave loans to individuals and businesses rather than to governments. Investments were used for the property market and the stock market instead of for agriculture or industry. The prices of property fell, and investors took money out of the economy, leading to a recession. Since then, the Tigers' economies have recovered, with stronger service and electronics industries. However, they have been overtaken by greater growth in other Asian countries, such as India and China.

Government aid

Following natural disasters, crop failures, or conflicts, people in poorer countries may need food, shelter, or new infrastructure that their countries cannot afford. Government aid is the help given by richer governments to poorer countries. Aid can include food rations for immediate benefit, and farming equipment or building expertise for long-term assistance.

Aid is not a loan to be repaid, but donors often benefit. For example, one country might offer to build a dam to give farmers access to irrigation water as long as businesses, equipment, and experts from their country can build the dam. It is estimated that 80 percent of the value of U.S. aid given to Africa is spent on U.S. businesses, such as building contractors.

■ The U.S. government gave aid in the form of food to victims of flash floods in Pakistan in 2010.

The financial industry

The financial industry that controls the flow of money to pay for production, trading, and aid in the global economy has many parts. Central banks, such as the Federal Reserve in the United States, control foreign exchange and how much money is printed for a country. Main street commercial banks and credit unions keep savings and give loans to customers. Investment banks deal in bonds and trade in shares for businesses, and also help businesses merge and buy other businesses—for example, to own new products.

Investment banks work closely with pension funds (savings for retirement that grow through stock trading) and **hedge funds**. These are privately owned investment companies that take bigger risks than banks, such as buying property rather than just shares of stock. Many people think the global economic crisis was caused in part by hedge funds (see pages 28–29).

WHAT DO YOU THINK?

Imagine if a brand-new hospital was built in your country through aid, but no one could use it because your country could not afford medical supplies or pay for staff, and most people could not get to it anyway. This actually happened in Samoa. In other countries, corrupt leaders sometimes prevent aid reaching the people who need it.

Is there any purpose in giving aid if a country does not use it properly? Or should donors consider the aid they give more carefully?

HEDGING BETS

Hedge funds trade in anything they can make money from. Some trade in **derivatives**, which are a bit like bets on the future value of something. For example, a hedge fund might agree to buy cocoa beans at a certain price in the future in case the price goes up before then. They may then be able to sell the beans at a profit. In case the beans fall lower in price, the hedge fund also bets against losing money on cocoa derivatives! Hedging is also a way in which firms can protect themselves against price changes.

These traders in bright yellow jackets are buying and selling based on the future value of the goods being traded.

Global businesses

Some businesses operate in many countries at the same time, even though their headquarters are in one country. These are called **multinational corporations**. For example, the multinational Johnson & Johnson is based in the United States. It owns around 250 companies in 60 countries, making anything from contact lenses and replacement joints to baby powder. The Gap clothing business is another multinational corporation based in the United States. It produces textiles from 3,200 factories worldwide. Because multinationals work in so many countries, the countries often both import and export products from the same company!

One major advantage for multinationals in making profits is being able to manufacture goods in, or provide services from, countries where salaries are lower—and sometimes in special areas called export processing zones in the countries where they pay low tax. Another advantage is using the specialized skills of different regions. For example, the call centers for the British communication company BT are in India because there is a large, highly educated workforce there that accepts lower salaries than those in the United Kingdom. The advantage for host countries are ready-made, successful businesses offering jobs, but in a global economy one country can easily lose out if another can provide even cheaper labor for the multinational.

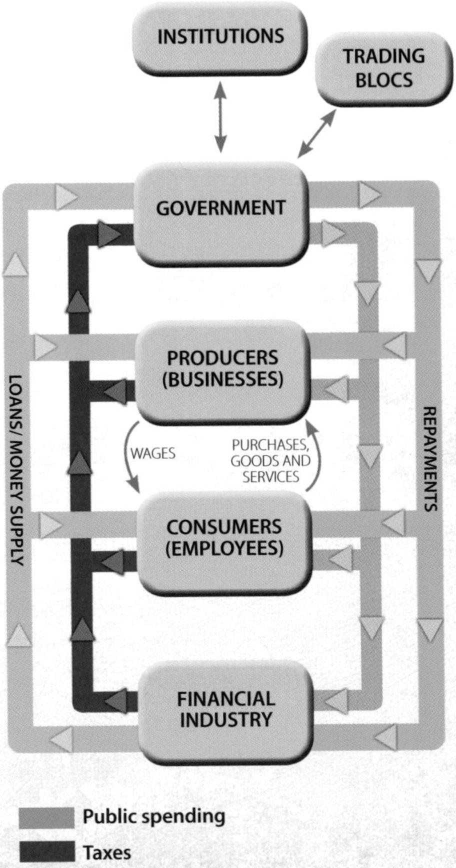

■ This diagram shows how all of the sectors of an economy are connected.

CASE STUDY

Bananas

Bananas are the fourth most valuable export crop in the world. Countries in the European Union mainly get their bananas from small, family-owned plantations in the Caribbean islands such, as Dominica and St. Vincent. This is partly because countries such as the United Kingdom used to have colonies in the islands. The United States gets most bananas from giant plantations owned by big corporations, including Chiquita, in Latin American countries (Spanish-speaking countries in Central and South America) such as Honduras and Guatemala. These bananas are cheaper to produce in large quantities than those in the Caribbean.

In the early 1990s, to protect the Caribbean industry, the European Union tried to restrict how many Latin American bananas could be imported. In 1997, the WTO ruled that European Union countries should buy more of their bananas from suppliers in Latin America to ensure free trade. The case was brought to the WTO by the U.S. government at the request of Chiquita. The company is based in Cincinnati, Ohio, but it has thousands of workers in Latin America. It was run by Carl Lindner who was an important contributor of money to the Republican Party. This is an example of the political influence of corporations over governments in the global economy.

"Many complicated agreements exist, and determine which countries may export bananas to which markets. However, the biggest problem is that developed countries are continually searching for the cheapest bananas."

Rebecca Cohen, *Science Creative Quarterly*, 2008

HOW DOES THE GLOBAL ECONOMY AFFECT FINANCES?

Imagine you are much older and receiving a pension. This is a regular payment based on money you saved, or an employer contributed, during your working life. The pension fund that pays your money invests in shares in businesses globally, so your payments are related to the success of anything from copper mines in Africa to supermarkets in Germany. These businesses may have received loans from banks or businesses worldwide. The interconnectedness of the financial industry, businesses, governments, and individuals across the world means that there are both positive and negative financial impacts for everyone.

A global economy means that recognizable luxury brands such as Bentley cars are in demand and available for sale from dealers worldwide, such as this one in Moscow, Russia.

CASE STUDY

Maldives

The Maldive Islands are isolated in the Indian Ocean south of India. Their GDP is 179th in the world. There are few domestic industries because of the lack of farmland and resources. Without the chance to be involved in the global economy, it would struggle economically. Fishing and tourism are the two main industries, and both rely on the global economy. The traditional fishing industry was on a very small scale and based on local consumption. Today, it accounts for the majority of the country's earnings from export goods. Most of the fish exported is valuable skipjack tuna which is generally sold to foreign companies for processing. Tuna is sold fresh (transported in refrigerated ships), canned, or dried.

Around 40 percent of Maldivian workers are in the tourism industry, which contributes around one-third of its GDP and nearly two-thirds of its foreign exchange. The tourism industry in the Maldives began in 1972 with the opening of the first, simple island resort on Malé island. It increased after the first international airport was built in 1981 and when the Maldivian government encouraged foreign investment in the country. By 2010, the annual number of tourists to the Maldives had risen to over 600,000.

Positive impacts

There are many benefits of the global economy. Foreign trade brings essential income to less-developed countries. For instance, Bangladesh, which in the past relied on agriculture for exports, is now a major producer of sewn garments for the global fashion industry. Foreign investment in industries to improve exports not only increases the number of jobs, but may also improve the infrastructure and encourage economic growth of other industries.

The Brazilian company Vale is investing millions to develop coal mining in the economically deprived Zambezi valley in Mozambique. This has involved improving the local power supply to aid mining, and providing a railway linking the valley with a port for exporting the coal. The success of the development has encouraged other companies from India and other countries to invest in Mozambique, whose GDP is too low to invest in the area itself.

Negative impacts

The interconnected nature of the global economy also has many negative financial impacts. Sometimes whole economies can rely too much on one industry, so they struggle when that industry suffers. For example, following the Indian Ocean tsunami, tourism infrastructure, such as hotels, were damaged, and tourist bookings were cancelled in many countries ranging from Thailand to the Maldives. In the Maldives alone, tourism income fell by $187 million between 2004 and 2005, which is around one-tenth of its GDP.

The failure of one industry can cause problems in related ones. For example, most British coal mines closed down during the 1980s and 1990s. This was partly because cheaper coal could be imported from countries such as Australia to run British power plants. With miners out of work, businesses near the mines, ranging from new car lots to real estate agents, also closed down.

Rows of boarded-up shops are a sign that the economy of an entire area is suffering.

> **"When the IMF and the World Bank force a country to cut wages, lay off workers, produce for export instead of the needs of their own people, and sell off public property ... that's called 'economic reform.'"**
>
> **Robert Naiman, senior policy analyst at the Center for Economic and Policy Research, 1999**

Outside control

As we have seen, the global economy is controlled partly by global institutions, businesses, and the financial industry. Sometimes the outside control of their activities can greatly influence economies. For example, banks may offer loans with low interest rates to people who cannot afford them in order to make profits (but see pages 28–31 to read an account of how this can backfire). In the past, the World Bank has been accused of making loans for development that do not actually help many people—for example, by lending money to build expensive hydroelectric dams or to set up farming industries in dry regions with too little water for filling reservoirs or for irrigation.

On the world stock markets, **commodities** such as oil or food are traded all the time, so they have fluctuating prices. Trade in commodity values (see page 21) to make profits can result in wildly varying prices, with consequences for regional and national economies. For example, vanilla is a major export crop in Madagascar. Most vanilla trade happens electronically in the commodities market rather than between individual traders. When a hurricane damaged vanilla crops in Madagascar in 2000, traders thought vanilla would be in short supply so vanilla prices rose rapidly on the commodities market. This encouraged growers to borrow money to plant more vanilla vines, not only in Madagascar, but also in Uganda, India, and Indonesia. There was then so much vanilla for sale that commodity prices fell by 98 percent. Some vanilla farmers faced economic ruin as they could not repay their loans.

The global economic crisis, 2007–2010

In February 2007, news stories started to appear about banks having big financial losses related to the housing market. This was the start of what became a global economic crisis. As the story unfolded, major players in the financial industry went bankrupt. Others were only saved by governments giving them money, and even whole nations needed to borrow money to protect their economies.

Causes of the crisis in the United States

In the 1990s, the construction industry in the United States grew because it built more homes, and the financial industry grew by lending money to people to buy them. Also, prices continued to rise, meaning people had to get bigger loans. Banks usually lend money to people, businesses, or even countries based on their **credit rating**. This is a measure of how easily they can repay loans in future, based on how well they have repaid loans in the past and how much money they earn. In the period before the crisis, many banks gave mortgages to people with poor credit who would normally not have gotten mortgages. These are called **sub-prime mortgages**. Why would they do this?

Basically, the banks sold the loans, and the financial risk, on to others! Rather than lend the money from bank funds, the banks sold bonds worth the value of the house to investment banks and hedge funds. These investors made money by trading the bonds on the market. The banks received house repayments and fees from investors in return for setting up the bonds. The result was that banks tried to sell more and more new mortgages for larger and larger amounts.

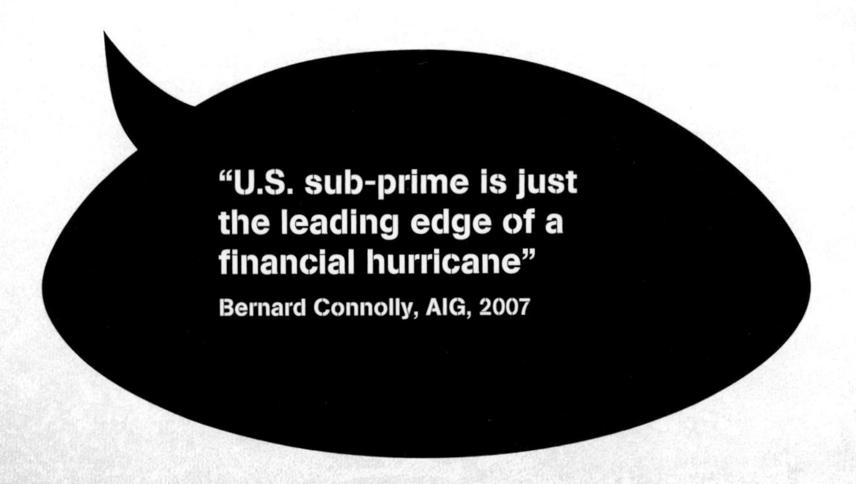

During the global economic crisis in 2008, employees of Lehman Brothers bank lost their jobs.

One way the banks encouraged people to take out sub-prime mortgages was by offering low repayments for the first few years. The repayments rose after that, and many people could not afford them. The banks then demanded repayment of the sum they had borrowed. This is called **foreclosure**. For most people, foreclosure meant that their homes were repossessed (taken back) by banks.

Spreading problems

As more and more houses were repossessed, so the value of all homes dropped because there were so many houses for sale. Banks were getting less money from mortgage customers but still had to make payments on bond loans. Many banks started to run out of money.

In 2008, the massive investment bank Lehman Brothers went bankrupt. Other giants, including the mortgage company Fannie Mae, only survived because the U.S. government lent them money. In 2008, the U.S. Congress agreed to give $700 billion to the banks as a bail out. The reason was that, if the banks were not supported by the government, foreign investors would lose trust in the U.S. economy, not lend to anyone, and the exchange rate of the dollar and other currencies may have gone down.

The problem goes global

The interconnectedness of the global economy meant that the problem soon went global. For example, British banks whose income depended on the success of investors with sub-prime bonds in the U.S. started to lose money. The British government gave over $60 billion to bail them out. Countries across the European Union took similar measures to save their banks in 2008 and 2009.

Investment banks and governments in countries including the United States suddenly had less money to invest overseas. For example, in 2007–2008, foreign investment in India was worth around $20.5 billion. This fell to around $11.5 billion in 2008–2009. Demand for many goods and services fell because people had less money and could not borrow any. Other factors made the situation worse, such as the rising price of oil. This caused an increase not only in costs of fuel for vehicles, but also of food and other goods requiring transportation. Many businesses struggled. Share values on global stock markets fell.

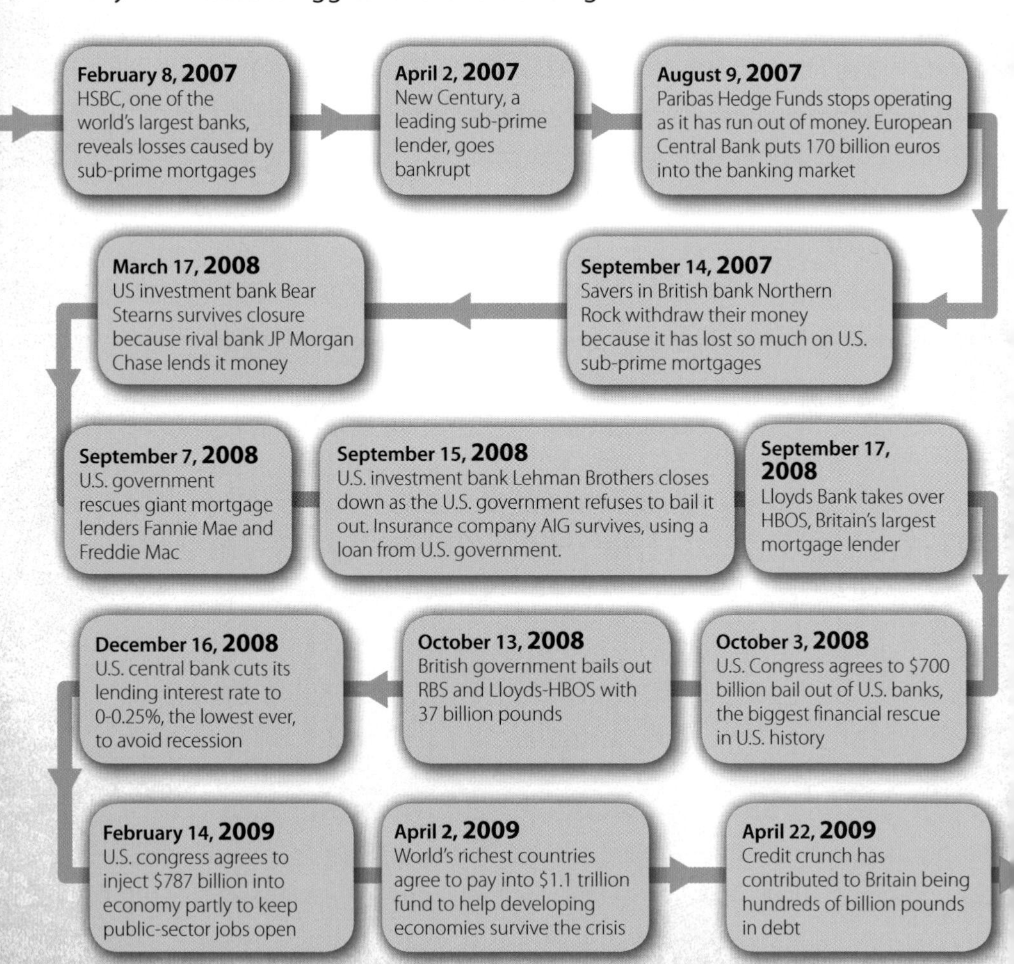

■ Greeks take to the streets in protest against austerity measures in February 2011.

Credit problems

Because they had to deal with unpaid debts from sub-prime mortgages, many banks became reluctant to lend money or give credit. This was called the **credit crunch**, and its effects were still being felt in 2011. The crunch affected people on different scales. Individuals had difficulty getting mortgages. Most faced increased taxes as governments tried to bring more money into central banks. Businesses found it difficult to borrow money to expand or to buy raw materials.

Countries whose growth relied more on borrowing than money made from industries struggled badly. The Greek government, for example, had borrowed heavily to pay for growth in public-sector jobs and improved infrastructure, as well as to ensure the success of the 2004 Olympics. When the economic crisis struck, more Greeks received public benefits and fewer could pay taxes, so the country struggled to pay its debts. With a low credit rating, investors lent less, and debts built to €300 billion ($420 billion).

The European Union and International Monetary Fund pledged a bail-out loan that had to be repaid over three years. To meet the repayments, the Greek government announced **austerity measures**, or national cost-cutting regulations. These included increases in tax (as well as tax on fuel), freezes in public-sector pay, and even the sale of some small Greek islands! This caused huge protests throughout Greece. Problems in Greece created ripples through the European Union. For example, Ireland, which had previously had one of the fastest growing economies in Europe, also sought a bail out (see page 17).

HUMAN IMPACTS OF THE GLOBAL ECONOMY

The global economy has the power to transform people's lives for the better, from access to new foods and culture, to new work opportunities. Equally, many people's lives have been thrown into turmoil by the world markets.

CULTURAL GAINS AND LOSSES

Cultures can change as a result of the global economy and **globalization**. For example, the spread of Western media has changed expectations in many countries toward greater freedom of speech and equal rights for all, such as access to education and work for women. Some people argue that such interconnectedness is, in some cases, causing cultural differences to be gradually lost. For example, access to MTV and other satellite stations, and to the internet, have globalized hip-hop music, which originated among poor African Americans in U.S. cities. In parts of countries, such as in China and Brazil today, these modern forms of music are displacing traditional music.

In some cases, there are backlashes against globalization. For example, the Slow Food movement started in Italy in 1986. It was part of an attempt to stop a McDonald's fast-food restaurant opening in Rome, and to support and defend good, locally sourced, seasonal food. Today, the organization is itself global, but it promotes distinct cuisines, family farms rather than industrial ones, and gardening skills.

The global economy has helped the spread of technology, such as this solar cooker in use in southwest China. Using solar cookers reduces the time families need to spend searching for wood for fuel and reduces the expense of buying other fuels to cook with.

New lives

The global economy has given many people new expectations of life. Consumers entering supermarkets may be faced with a choice of goods to buy from all over the world as a result of global trading. For example, chili is widely used in Indian, Chinese, and Thai food even though it originated in Central and South America. Competition for trade has made consumer technology, such as televisions and laptops, much cheaper than they were in the past in many countries.

Cheap travel is now commonplace, with expanding global airlines, so people can easily travel from country to country. Labor practices can also become more efficient. For example, the European and U.S. car industries improved their rate of production and raised profits by basing their factories and workforce organization on those in Japan and other Asian countries.

The impact on lives goes beyond trade. Expansion of global internet and mobile communications means that information and knowledge is spreading faster than ever before in history. Around 70 percent of the global population has a cell phone contract! Political revolutions in Tunisia and Egypt in 2011 were spread and organized partly using such technology.

Problems for workers

The global economy has many negative impacts on people, especially workers. Producing cheap goods on a large scale usually requires labor-saving technology, which is expensive, or the alternative—using cheap mass labor. The latter is easy to find in poorer regions and in less developed countries eager to experience economic growth.

Factories keep costs to a minimum partly by paying extremely low wages that keep workers in poverty. They also save money by providing poor working conditions. These include long working shifts for workers, limited bathroom breaks, no paid overtime or holidays, and unsafe working conditions, such as workers using dangerous machinery with no protective clothing. This type of factory is often called a **sweatshop**.

■ Many children are illegally employed in sweatshops around the world, such as this Indian match factory. Their working conditions are a consequence of demand for ever-cheaper goods in the global economy.

CASE STUDY

Bhopal

Possibly the worst industrial accident in history happened on December 3, 1984, when a leak in Union Carbide's insecticide factory in Bhopal, India, released a cloud of almost 50 tons of poisonous gases over the city. The gas killed 3,500 people instantly and forced tens of thousands to flee the city. Since then, over 20,000 people have died and thousands more suffer from breathing problems, cancers, blindness, and other health problems caused by exposure to the gases or from drinking poisoned water. The water was poisoned when harmful chemicals in the factory, which was closed following the accident, seeped into the soil.

Investigations into the accident established that the factory had insufficient safety procedures and staff, which meant that the leak was not found in time. Union Carbide paid $470 million in compensation to victims, which was insufficient to compensate families of people who had died or to pay for healthcare for those still suffering. After years of court cases, seven Indian operation managers from the factory were jailed in 2010. However, the former chairman of Union Carbide, Warren Anderson, refuses to return to India from the United States in order to face charges that state he was at least partly to blame for the disaster.

WHAT DO YOU THINK?

Before the global economy expanded, poor people now working in sweatshops in countries such as Mexico, India, and China probably would have had no work at all. Is it better to have steady employment, whatever the conditions, than no work? Does sweatshop work have any other benefits, such as training?

Moving to work

Globally, there are around 214 million **migrants**. People move to other countries for many different reasons. The main ones are to avoid persecution or conflict, and to find work and earn more money. Often workers send most of their earnings home to their families. In 2009, economic migrants sent home over $421 billion. Most of this went to poorer, less developed countries where wages are generally very low and there are fewer work opportunities. Migrants benefit through wages, and host countries benefit because migrants fill gaps in their workforce and often take lower paid work that their citizens may not want to do. For example, many Bangladeshi and Indian migrants work in the rich countries in the Middle East, usually as construction workers or domestic workers.

■ Chinese rural migrant workers in the city of Shenyang in 2010 hold signs advertising the type of work they can do.

Most countries limit the numbers of legal immigrants to ensure their citizens get the jobs they want. However, the lure of possible riches in more developed countries means that there are vast numbers of illegal immigrants. In the United States, around 150,000 Mexicans enter the country illegally each year. They sneak over the border at night or in dangerous conditions hidden under goods in trucks. Both legal and illegal immigrants face many challenges, such as exploitation by employers and persecution by locals who fear their jobs are being taken.

Thai dairy farmers in 2005 dumped milk to protest the lack of government subsidies which would have made their milk cheap enough to compete with imported milk.

Food issues

The global export market means that farmers can specialize in crops for sale on the other side of the world rather than for local consumption. For example, many farmers in Burkina Faso, Africa, one of the world's poorest countries, grow green beans for sale in France and other European Union nations, especially during the winter when it is too cold to grow beans in European countries. However, with so much dependent on one perishable crop, Burkina Faso bean farmers make no money if a crop fails, or if an airplane for transporting the crop is delayed.

Like most farmers growing for export, Burkina Faso bean farmers face competition from other farmers worldwide, and this competition is not fair when prices are subsidized. For example, the U.S. government heavily subsidizes its farmers to produce cheap corn to make cattle feed or sweet syrup to add to foods. The farmers also export corn to Mexico, where it is the staple food, at lower prices than the locals can grow it for. This process is called **dumping**. Corn dumping between 1997 and 2005 cost Mexican farmers around $6.6 billion.

Export farm owners, with the financial backing of multinationals such as big supermarket chains, buy up productive land in countries to improve their export crops. For example, in some areas of Guatemala, the best farmland is covered with export plantations for coffee, biofuel crops, and sugar. Local farmers' crops regularly fail on the rest of the land, and they are too poor to buy food. Half of Guatemalan children under five do not have enough to eat.

ENVIRONMENTAL IMPACTS

Accessing raw materials, manufacturing, and transportation of goods all have an impact on the environment. **Deforestation** is just one of many negative impacts. Sometimes, however, the global economy can become a force for good in terms of environmental change.

Deforestation

Most deforestation happens in the tropics, and the biggest cause is agriculture. From the 1960s, Amazonian rain forests in Brazil have been cut down to make way for cattle ranches for beef exports. In recent times, trees have also been cleared to grow soybeans, which are in global demand for use in the food and chemical industries. Logging companies also cut down trees to provide wood and paper products. Farming and logging require roads to reach new areas of forest, leading to more deforestation.

When trees are cut down in Brazil to supply goods for the global economy, the environment is affected in several ways. Loss of trees means loss of habitat for thousands of plant and animal species. Without trees to protect land, soils can dry out and areas become desert. But the impact is more far-reaching. Deforestation changes weather patterns worldwide because trees normally absorb the greenhouse gases that fuel **global warming**.

A large patch of rain forest burns to make space for more farmland in Brazil.

Loss of natural resources

When a region supplies goods or services for the global economy, this can have an impact on other resources, such as water. In tourist resorts, a lot of water is used for hotel sanitation, cleaning, and other things such as swimming pools. In recent years, the number of golf courses at coastal resorts has increased rapidly, causing severe water shortages for locals. Tourism Concern points out that "An average golf course in a tropical country such as Thailand … uses as much water as 60,000 rural villages."

"We have seen water pressure dropping in the past years since the agro-exporters came, but if the water runs out and they leave, we will have no work and no water."

A Peruvian villager

CASE STUDY

Asparagus from Peru

Peru is the largest exporter of asparagus in the world, 95 percent of which is grown in the Ica valley. Growing asparagus has become big business in Peru, thanks to multimillion dollar investments by the World Bank since the 1990s. It has created around 10,000 jobs and improved the country's economy. But asparagus is a water-hungry crop, and big export farms are emptying local underground water supplies so quickly that the wells of families and small farms are drying up. Export farmers are paying more for water, and, while there are official limits on how much they can withdraw, many get around these limits by buying up farmland for greater access to more wells. And so local citizens are left with even less water.

Pollution

Pollution can be caused by businesses involved in the global economy in various ways. Electricity is an energy source that is vital for factory production, for example. Burning coal supplies about two-thirds of China's energy consumption. It releases sulfur and nitrogen dioxide gases into the atmosphere, which combine with water to form acid rain. Acid rain can damage wildlife and trees and pollute drinking water supplies. Effects are not always local. For example, acid rain originating from industries in the Ruhr industrial region of northern Germany has damaged forests up to 1,600 miles (1,000 kilometers) away in Scandinavia. Smoke and fumes from highway transportation and industry also affect human health. Worldwide, more deaths are linked to air pollution every year than to car accidents.

Mining and drilling for raw materials is a major cause of water pollution. The Gulf of Mexico oil spill in April 2010 was the largest ocean oil spill in history. It was caused by an explosion on the Deepwater Horizon oil rig, run by the energy company BP. Oil does not dissolve in water. It forms a thick, floating layer on the surface that not only covers coasts, but also chokes and poisons marine animals. The spill brought unemployment and hardship to local fishing and tourism industries. Its long-term ecological effects are still not known.

Dirty water from factories pollutes nearby rivers.

Global warming

The global economy relies on transport networks to fly, drive, or ship raw materials, goods, and people between countries. In addition to causing air pollution, vehicle emissions are also a significant contributor to global warming. Proof of this was seen in 2009 when the reduction in economic activity caused by the economic crisis of 2008 also brought the sharpest drop in emissions in 40 years, with estimates ranging from 3 to 10 percent.

WHAT DO YOU THINK?

BP is held responsible for the Gulf of Mexico spill because its well safety systems failed. The U.S. government expects it to clean up the oil pollution. The U.S. company Dow Corning, which now owns Union Carbide, has still not cleaned up the site of the Bhopal accident (see page 35) which is poisoning the local water supply.

Should Dow Corning be held responsible for an accident that happened decades ago? Is it better for India to try to make Dow Corning accountable, or to encourage it to make further investments that could create Indian jobs? Does it make a difference that one accident happened in the United States and another in India?

"Scientists say a rise of six degrees in average global temperatures would have cataclysmic and irreversible consequences for the planet and threaten the basis of human civilization."

Greenpeace

Positive impacts

Many businesses worldwide are careful to minimize the impact of their economic activities on the environment, partly because it can save money. For example, in the city of Bogotá, Colombia, soil and agricultural chemicals washing off deforested areas were polluting freshwater supplies. The Bavaria drinks company needs fresh water to make its products, but its water bill rose by 35 percent between 2004 and 2009 due to extra costs of water treatment. Bavaria saved money using technology that helped process drinks using less water. It also partly funded a Nature Conservancy project in the Chingaza National Park above Bogotá, where most of its water comes from. This project planted trees and fenced off cattle from rivers to help stop soil from washing into rivers. With improving water quality for Bavaria and residents in Bogotá, water treatment should cost several million dollars less each year.

Reducing environmental impacts may also improve the image of businesses. Consumers reading news about environmental damage may boycott, or refuse to buy, goods from a particular company. For example, Asia Pulp and Paper (APP) is one of the world's largest paper manufacturers. In 2004, a large group of Chinese hotels discovered that some of the wood they used to make paper was illegally logged from protected areas of forest in China. The hotels boycotted APP products and APP stopped the illegal logging.

■ In place of conventional fossil fuels—to reduce the environmental impact of cars—there is growing global use of biodiesel, here recycled from used vegetable oil..

CASE STUDY

McDonald's food for fuel

Like any fast-food establishment, McDonald's produces waste that is mostly organic, or food, waste. This is a waste of money in terms of the cost of the food thrown away. It also costs the company money because they have to dispose of it. There are also environmental costs. Food waste that ends up in landfills releases methane, a powerful greenhouse gas. Waste that is incinerated, or burned, causes air pollution. McDonald's restaurants in Switzerland have developed a way to recycle food waste that benefits both the environment and the business.

McDonald's restaurants in Switzerland have a separate bin for organic waste materials. A company called Kompogas collects this organic waste and ferments it into a biogas, a type of gas made from dead plant material that can be burned to make heat like other forms of gas or oil. This biogas is then used for heating and to fuel the company's own biogas truck that collects the waste. The biogas truck saves about 2,400 gallons (10,000 liters) of diesel fuel a year. The amount of biogas that can be produced with the organic waste from all Swiss McDonald's restaurants is about the same as that needed to fuel the truck. McDonald's shareholders benefit, too. Compared with the former incineration costs, the Swiss restaurants now pay 60 percent less for the disposal of their organic waste.

CHANGES IN THE GLOBAL ECONOMY

The interconnected global economy is very complicated. As we have seen, there are winners and losers in all parts of it. But there are big changes in progress, from who is lending money to how goods are being produced without exploiting workers or damaging the environment.

Different lenders

In recent years, there has been some shift in economic power away from the United States and big European Union economies such as Germany. Today, some of the fastest growing economies are in Brazil, Russia, India, and China (BRIC countries). BRIC governments and private corporations today lend four times as much as international institutions such as the International Monetary Fund (IMF). In turn, many companies want to invest in the growing BRIC economies. Some vast multinational corporations are richer than certain countries. For example, Exxon Mobil energy company is worth more than Pakistan!

Microlending

The vast majority of people around the world with low incomes cannot get standard bank loans because their credit ratings are too low. Some people have no option but to go to moneylenders, who often charge very high interest. Others have access to microlending or microcredit. This type of money supply includes small-scale loans for poor people to help them escape poverty. Such loans are given by cooperative groups, banks, and charities working across Asia and Africa, but also by global micro-lending websites. On these websites, people apply for loans stating exactly what they want to use the money for. Based on this, investors can lend money directly. Investors specify how much interest they want in return on some of these sites, but on others, people invest without expecting profit.

CASE STUDY

Grameen Bank

The Grameen (or village) Bank is a microlending organization founded by Muhammed Yunus in Bangladesh in 1976. Yunus realized poor people remained in poverty because of a lack of money and banking services rather than lack of skills. Giving Bangladeshis access to loans would allow them to use their skills to raise themselves out of poverty. He started to lend money in the small village of Jobra. The idea soon spread, and now there are over 2,500 branches of Grameen Bank spread across the country.

Grameen promotes several ideas quite different from those of most banks. These include considering credit to be a human right, and giving credit based on trust and not based on how much wealth a person has. People take out Grameen loans by joining a group of borrowers which now totals over eight million—mostly women. The borrowers own the vast majority of the bank. Any loan has to be paid back in weekly or biweekly installments.

The interest rate people pay depends on their circumstances. For example, it is 20 percent for business loans but 0 percent for struggling members or homeless people. Since its creation, Grameen has lent around $10.2 billion, of which $9.2 billion has been repaid. In 2006, Yunus won the Nobel Peace Prize for his acts of economic and social development in Bangladesh. Grameen today advises similar microlending schemes in many countries, including Ethiopia and Peru.

A Grameen loan enabled this woman to set up a profitable rickshaw business in Bangladesh.

A better way of trading

There is growing access to information about conditions in sweatshops, environmental damage, and other problems in the global economy. Increasing numbers of consumers worldwide want to know about, and improve, the working conditions for people that produce the things they buy. They believe that businesses should take responsibility for the things they sell and promote the rights of workers and the protection of the environment.

Fair-trade workers at this cocoa cooperative in Ghana have a stake in the success of their products.

The **fair-trade** movement exists to ensure that workers get fair wages regardless of changes in world prices of commodities, currencies, and other aspects of the financial industry. Members of the Fairtrade Labeling Organizations International, such as the Britain-based Fairtrade Foundation, work with individuals, businesses, and organizations to improve the position of producers in poorer countries. They certify and allow fair-trade labeling of products ranging from bananas and chocolate to cotton and vacation resorts. A fair-trade price paid to a farmer, for example, includes a minimum price, below which production is not being adequately paid for, and a premium. The premium is invested in economic, social, and environmental development of their workers and families. For example, Mabale Growers' Tea Factory in Uganda has used the premium partly to construct sheds with concrete floors and tin roofs where farmers can store picked tea leaves and protect them from sun and rain before collection for processing at the factory.

CASE STUDY

Helping children using chocolate

Most cocoa used to make chocolate grows in tropical conditions in West African countries, including Ivory Coast and Ghana. It is mostly produced on large plantations and on numerous family farms. Children are forced to work on some plantations, weeding between cocoa trees and picking pods. They risk injury or sickness from machinery or exposure to pesticides. Sometimes these children are taken from villages in other countries, such as Mali, and sold to the farms. The use of child labor is a consequence of large chocolate companies demanding such cheap cocoa that farmers cannot afford to pay adult salaries.

Cadbury is a large chocolate manufacturer that is taking a lead in improving the cocoa trade. In 2010, it started to make its best-selling Dairy Milk bar using fair-trade cocoa for the United Kingdom, Australia, Canada, Ireland, and New Zealand markets. By the end of 2010, this amounted to around 350 million bars. The cocoa is mostly from the Kuapa Kokoo cooperative in Ghana, whose farms do not use child labor and instead pay fair salaries to adult workers. Cadbury is also investing in the farming communities it relies on in Ghana, Indonesia, and the Caribbean through the Cadbury Cocoa Partnership. For example, the partnership works with charities, such as Water Aid, to build freshwater wells in villages and to train teachers skilled in IT (information technology).

"I did not get any education, but I want my children to. Because of the fair-trade price, I can send them to school."

Laljibhai Narranbhai, fair trade cotton farmer

Sustainability

Global trade is encouraging the use of natural resources—such as water, forests, fisheries, and minerals—much faster than they can be regenerated, so there is a global drive toward being **sustainable**. This means using natural resources and energy in a way that does not harm the environment and that can be continued for a long time. This can be achieved in many ways. For example, logging companies can plant new trees to replace the ones they cut down; food producers can use biodegradable packaging instead of plastic; restaurants can recycle cooking oil for transport; and fishing quotas can be used to ensure areas of the ocean are not overfished.

Recycling waste

Recycling creates economic value from waste and reduces the environmental impact of making new goods from raw materials. But more developed countries often export waste to less developed countries where recycling is cheaper. For example, "e-waste," which includes old computers and TVs, is shipped to countries such as China and India where workers extract some of the precious metals used in the equipment. In addition to the environmental cost of transporting waste long distances, e-waste is often incinerated or broken up by hand, creating pollution, injuries, and health problems for workers. Globally, e-waste is increasing by over 44 million tons each year, making it a major sustainability issue.

WHAT DO YOU THINK?

A carbon tax is a tax some countries impose on businesses that use fossil fuels and release greenhouse gas emissions, which can damage the environment. The idea is that charging businesses for carbon dioxide emissions released during production will encourage them to pollute less and become more environmentally friendly.

Why would some countries not require such a tax? What will happen if not all countries charge carbon taxes?

Reclaiming metals, including gold from e-waste, shifts the environmental impact from gold mines to recycling centers worldwide.

Going local and staying global

In some countries, environmentalists are calling for people to buy and trade locally to reduce emissions from long-distance transportation that contributes to global warming. For example, if people in the United States bought home-grown apples rather than imported ones, the **food miles** clocked up for fruit sold in supermarkets would drop. However, this is not as simple as it seems.

The fuel used by individuals driving to supermarkets to buy food is more per person than the amount used by the large airplanes or ships that carry goods in bulk. In addition, production in less developed countries may also use less energy—for example, by using fewer agricultural machines. But the choice between local or global is not just about food miles. Sales, in more developed countries, of food grown and exported, from less developed countries, can help to relieve poverty worldwide.

"One person's waste can be another's raw material. The challenge of dealing with e-waste represents an important step in the transition to a green economy."

Konrad Osterwalder, United Nations

The need for change

The global economy benefits the richest countries, which dominate world trade, far more than less developed countries. In many cases, less developed countries provide cheap labor and raw materials, while profits are sent back to the country where the multinational is based. Multinationals may also take advantage of the lack of legal protection for workers concerning wages, working conditions, or safety to operate in a way they would not in their own country. Some people also see the global economy as a threat to the world's cultural diversity. They think that by spreading a capitalist, Western way of life in less developed countries, multinationals are also responsible for crushing local economies, traditions, and languages.

Critics, who highlight the negative impacts of the global economy, campaign to promote change. For example, in November 1999, protesters rioted and held rallies and marches in at least 20 countries against World Trade Organization (WTO) meetings in Seattle, where major governments met to discuss trading rules. In Turkey in 2009 and in Washington D.C. in 2010, protesters marched against the International Monetary Fund (IMF), which campaigners accuse of directing global economies to the detriment of the world's poor. Developing countries make up nearly half of the world economy, but only have about one-third of the votes in the IMF.

Many people believe that the global economy benefits a minority at the expense of the majority. These protestors at the IMF meeting in Istanbul, 2009, risked arrest to make their views known.

Tackling poverty

The need for change is partly being addressed by charitable foundations, such as the Bill and Melinda Gates Foundation. Bill Gates made Microsoft into the world's largest software company and then became the world's richest man. He and his wife used this wealth to set up the foundation to help poor countries. It pays for health and immunization programs, builds schools, and helps small businesses. For example, the Gates Foundation is investing $10 billion between 2010 and 2020 to research, develop, and deliver vaccines to combat diseases such as malaria and tuberculosis.

There are also global initiatives for change. The UN's Millennium Development Goals are a set of goals for tackling extreme poverty agreed to by world leaders in 2000 and to be met by 2015. They include developing fairer trading and financial systems that address the special needs of the least developed countries. It calls for the barriers of protectionism to be removed by richer countries so the least developed countries can more easily export their products. It also aims to reduce, or even cancel debt, for example, from the World Bank or other development loans, to allow poor countries to spend their money on development instead.

"It is not in the United Nations that the Millennium Development Goals will be achieved. They have to be achieved in each of its Member States, by the joint efforts of their governments and people."

Kofi Annan, Secretary-General of the United Nations, 1997–2006

OUR SHARED ECONOMIC FUTURE

The global economy in 2011 was just starting to come out of the biggest financial crisis for decades. Although many banks and parts of the financial industry started to make big profits again, other industries, government, and individuals worldwide were still struggling with problems such as falling profits, zero economic growth, and unemployment. So what are the future trends, events, and challenges that face the global economy?

Growing economies

In 2010, the World Bank published a report saying that Africa "could be on the brink of economic take-off," much the way China was 30 years ago and India was 20 years ago. An important reason is that Africa is rich in natural resources such as minerals and oil. Some of the most eager investors are India and China, who are buying up farmland and investing in mines across the continent in order to supply their own economies. But different countries worldwide are racing to find more resources—for example, by increasing oil production in deep water in the Arctic and, in the future, in Antarctic waters.

At the annual meeting of the Africa Development Bank in Shanghai, China in 2007, Chinese companies operating in Africa were encouraged to be sensitive to local conditions and give back to communities in order to succeed in a continent that is a growing Chinese investment target.

Population changes

Experts predict that, by 2050, the global population will be around 9 billion—that is around a third more than it is today. The greater demand for limited resources, such as fossil fuels and water, will cause rising prices, stall economic growth, and create resource conflicts between individuals, regions, and countries. In 2011, there was already tension over water sharing by countries, such as Egypt and Ethiopia, through which the Nile River runs. The increasing trend of people moving from rural areas to live in cities could put greater pressure on local resources.

Changes in the makeup of populations will also have significant effects. For example, many countries, especially in the more developed world, have growing populations of older people. This is due to improvements in healthcare and due to fewer children being born. This will put pressure on economies with people working longer before retirement and on governments and the financial industry in paying pensions.

Climate changes

Most scientists agree that changing climates resulting from global warming will massively affect economies around the world. Increasing frequency of severe weather events, flooding, and droughts is already having a major impact, especially on food production. Technological solutions for producing more food in changing climates will help. These include developing new crops that grow with less water and are more resistant to pests and improving irrigation methods. However, some areas where economic growth relies on a good climate and fertile soil may struggle. Experts predict that farmland in southern Europe and northern Africa may become too dry for large-scale food production, but rising temperatures may help other regions.

WHAT DO YOU THINK?

Global warming may thaw rich frozen soils of Siberia that could be used for large-scale farming, but the release of methane, a greenhouse gas previously trapped in the soil, would also increase global warming. Do the benefits to world food production outweigh the negative impacts?

Technological changes

The future of the global economy will also depend on changing technology. The global computing industry did not exist before the 1980s. Now computers are integral to all industries, from controlling robots making cars in factories to handling the money supply in the financial industry. Computers have changed the way we access, share, and distribute music, books, and other media. The rate of change of technology could have great implications for future jobs and service industries. For example, there could be robot surgeons and soldiers and very few store clerks because more and more people shop online.

The growth in **green technology** could have an even greater effect on economies. Experts estimate that China would have to use three times the amount of energy used by the United States to match its standard of living, due to its enormous population. The Chinese government pledged over $221 billion in 2009 to expand green technology production and research. Green technology includes using solar and wind power to make electricity instead of coal or gas-fired power plants. China already has the largest solar water heating market in the world and 80 wind turbine manufacturers.

The other great green technological challenge is developing alternatives to oil in vehicles to slow the use of scarce fossil fuels and slow down emissions of greenhouse gases. The automobile industry, in particular in the United States, Japan, and Germany, is investing heavily in hydrogen power. This kind of technology involves vehicles powered by special batteries, called fuel cells, which are refueled with liquid hydrogen. Use of hydrogen in vehicles is currently limited, but, once hydrogen can be produced more cheaply, some scientists believe it will be the start of a new hydrogen economy.

"This is really the opportunity of a lifetime to tackle such an important energy problem that will have tremendous impact in the future of our society."

Professor Peidong Yang, Berkeley Lab Motor Company, 2000

Increasing use of green technology, such as hydrogen fuel cells, could have a profound effect on the global economy in terms of increasing jobs and lessening the environmental impact of people and their businesses on the planet.

CASE STUDY

Artifical leaves for fuel

Plants make food using photosynthesis, a process that combines carbon dioxide and water using the Sun's energy to make sugars. In 2005, scientists at Berkeley Lab in California set up the Helios Project to develop artificial leaves for making fuels. The leaves are special solar cells—thin layers of materials that produce electricity when sunlight strikes them. Tiny crystals between the layers use this power to change carbon dioxide and water into fuel. It has been calculated that covering 90,625 square miles (235,000 square kilometers) of land with artificial leaves—an area twice that of Cuba—in the United States could generate far more energy every year than the nation currently consumes.

In 2010, the Helios Project was pledged money for research and development of the cells as part of a $122 million sum given by the U.S. government to find ways of generating fuels directly from sunlight.

FACT FILE

All about GDP

Gross domestic product (GDP) is probably the most important way we compare economies. It is measured in three ways:

1. Output: the value of all goods and services from the different industries. To find this out, thousands of businesses are surveyed by economists.
2. Expenditure: value of goods and services, and investments purchased by governments, businesses, organizations, and households. It includes value of exports minus value of imports, too.
3. Income: profits and salaries earned by people, businesses, and governments.

The number from each measure should be about the same, but governments often figure out GDP using all three measures.

The GDP estimates for different countries in the global economy are very different. For example, the U.S. GDP is about 1,000 times larger than that of the tiny Pacific island of Tuvalu (see graph on opposite page). This is a result of:

- its size and geographical position;
- the wealth of government, banks, and institutions available for investment in businesses, education, and social support; and
- access to natural resources.

It is also a consequence of a larger population and workforce.

A larger population does not mean an individual in a country makes more money. GDP per capita (per person) is basically the GDP divided by the number of people in a country. It does not mean that every individual earns this much. In reality, there may be a few very rich people and large numbers of very poor people. China has the largest population of any country and the second largest GDP, due to its manufacturing goods for its own people and for businesses and countries worldwide. However, the GDP per capita is about one-seventh of that of the United States. This is because it is divided up among more people. There are other factors, too, such as low salaries in the country.

GDP of the 10 richest and 6 poorest countries

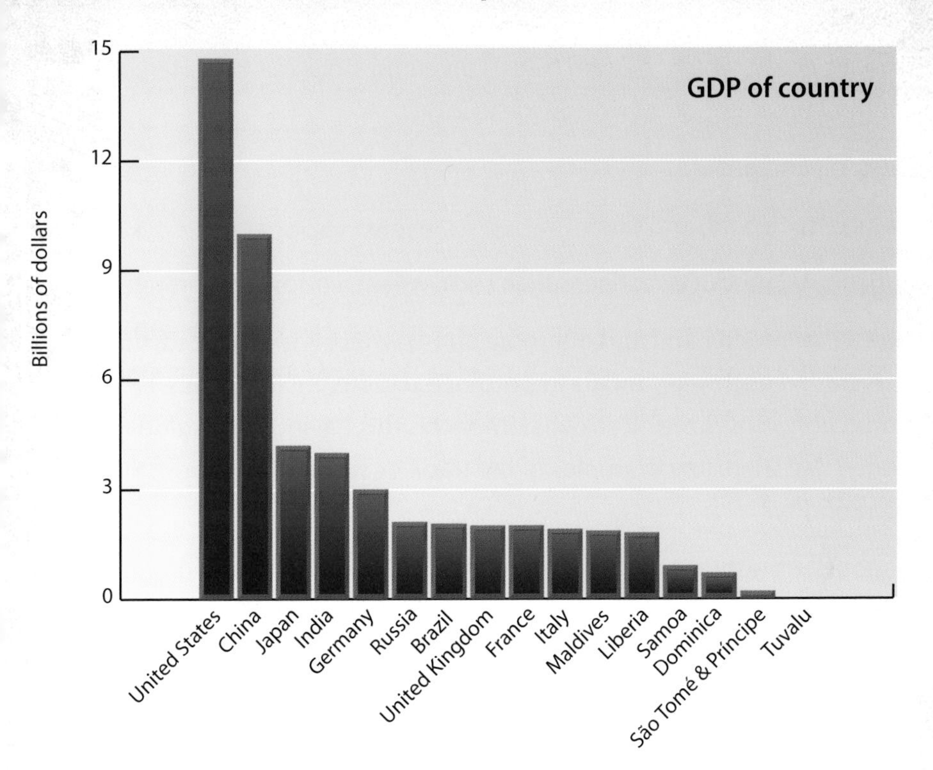

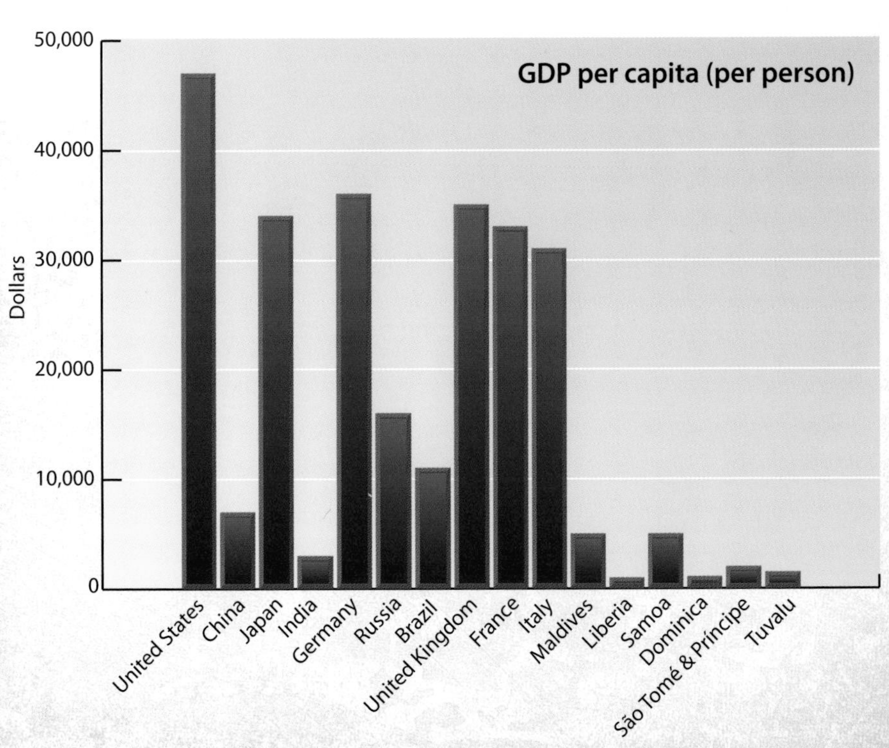

Research world commodities

Commodities are resources that are in demand, in good supply, and have a particular price at which they are traded on world stock markets. Here are the most popular commodities worldwide in 2011:

- Fuels: oil and gas
- Metals: steel, gold, and silver
- Agricultural products: coffee, sugar, corn, wheat, cotton, and orange juice

Choose a commodity and find out more about where it is produced, how much is traded each year, and its importance to different industries. Is its production subsidized? If so, what impact is this having in the global economy? Are there any examples of fair trade or sustainable production of the commodity?

Very important resources such as water, solar power, and carbon (in carbon dioxide gas that contributes to global warming) are not widely traded commodities. Find out more about the economic importance of these commodities and how this might change in the future.

Gold is a commodity that has consistently increased in value over recent years.

OPPOSING VIEWS ON AID

"$600 billion in aid to Africa over the past 45 years, and over that time period there's basically been zero rise in living standards."

William Easterly, Professor of Economics, New York University

"In 2002, we had perhaps 50,000 people on anti-retroviral treatment [for AIDS symptoms] in Africa. Thanks to aid, we now have well over a million people on anti-retroviral treatment within just five years."

John McArthur, Center for Globalization and Sustainable Development at the Earth Institute, Columbia University, 2007

GLOSSARY

austerity measure way that governments reduce public spending and increase taxes to raise funds during economic difficulties

bankruptcy inability to pay any money owed

capital-intensive requiring the investment of large sums of money

Caribbean island region to the east of Mexico and Central America and northeast of South America

commodity anything that can be bought or sold. The term is usually used in an economic context.

credit crunch when banks lend very little money, at high interest rates

credit rating estimate of how risky it is to lend money to an individual, organization, business, or government, based on how they have repaid loans in the past

deforestation cutting forest or woodland down to access land or resources beneath it

demand in economics, the willingness to purchase services and goods

depression in economics, a reduction in GDP by over 10 percent of its normal value for a year or more

derivative asset whose value is derived from one or more underlying assets

dumping practice of exporting goods to a country where they are much less expensive than domestically produced goods of the same type

European Union (EU) a political and economic organization of European countries

export movement and sale of goods or services out of one country into another

fair trade when producers of goods or services, from chocolate to vacations, get a fair wage and work in safe conditions, in ways that are sustainable and benefit the environment

food miles distance that food travels from farm to table, used as a measure of the environmental impact of transportation of goods

foreclosure legal process by which an owner's right to a property is terminated, usually due to a failure to keep up with mortgage payments

foreign exchange system of making payments from one country to another by converting a value from one currency to another, using agreed exchange rates. For example, $1.60 is exchanged for around €1.20 or £1.

free trade trading without restriction by government

globalization process of integration between economies and societies all over the world

global warming worldwide increase in temperature widely believed to be caused by storage of heat by gases including carbon dioxide, which is released into the atmosphere by machines that burn fuels

goods products that can be physically delivered to, and owned by, a purchaser, such as bananas or a car

green technology technology, such as wind turbines or solar cells, that help conserve the environment (for example, by reducing pollution or reducing the use of oil and other fuels)

gross domestic product (GDP) measure of the current production of an economy

hedge fund high-risk investment company for wealthy investors

import movement and sale of goods or services into one country from another

Industrial Revolution period from the 18th to 19th centuries during which there was rapid economic change in Europe, the United States, and other countries, caused by industrial growth and new technologies

infrastructure essential facilities and services for a functioning economy, such as highways and hospitals

interest fee paid by one person or organization to another, either for borrowing or for storing money

International Monetary Fund (IMF) international organization that promotes trade between nations and oversees the global economy

land-intensive requiring a large amount of land

loan sum of money that someone borrows and pays back

migrant person who moves from one country or region to another, often for economic benefit or safety

multinational corporation business that operates in many countries at the same time

plantation large area or estate where crops are grown, often for sale in another country rather than locally

protectionism policy in which governments use political and financial means to help their own industries; the opposite of free trade

public sector part of society supported or controlled by the government rather than by private businesses or individuals

quota restriction on the amount of goods that can be imported

recession in economics, a reduction in GDP over six months

resource useful or necessary substances such as coal, water, land, or steel

service type of product providing a support or activity for others, such as a haircut, dental treatment, or restaurant meal

share equal part of the value of a business or organization that can rise or fall depending on demand

stock market place where shares and other financial products are traded

sub-prime mortgage house-purchase loan given to someone who has a poor credit rating and would not be able to repay the mortgage

subsidy money given by the state to help an industry

supply in economics, the amount available to customers

sustainable meeting needs now and into the future without causing environmental damage or harming resource supplies

sweatshop factory where people work in poor conditions for low wages

World Bank international organization lending money to poorer countries to promote development and free trade

World Trade Organization (WTO) forum for governments to negotiate trade agreements and to settle any disputes

FURTHER INFORMATION

Books

Connolly, Sean. *International Aid and Loans* (World Economy Explained). Mankato, Minn.: Amicus, 2011.

Fay, Gail. *Economies Around the World* (Understanding Money). Chicago: Heinemann-Raintree, 2011.

Healy, Aaron. *Making the Trade: Stocks, Bonds, and Other Investments* (The Global Marketplace). Chicago: Heinemann-Raintree, 2010.

Hynson, Colin. *New Global Economies* (The World Today). North Mankato, Minn.: Sea to Sea Publications, 2010.

Bowden, Rob. *Trade* (The Global Village). New York: M. Evans and Company, 2008.

Websites

A useful site with different sections that help explain basic economics, including "The Stock Market," "What Banks Do," "How the Internet has Changed Buying and Selling," and "The Importance of Trade":
www.socialstudiesforkids.com/subjects/economics.htm

Visit the following site to learn more about the members, organization, or activities of the European Union, the largest economy on Earth:
europa.eu/about-eu/index_en.htm

If you are interested in issues about food production and the benefits of fair trade, then visit the following site:
www.oxfam.org.uk/coolplanet/kidsweb/food.htm

The following educational BBC site includes an excellent summary of globalization:
www.bbc.co.uk/schools/gcsebitesize/geography/industry/globalisation_rev1.shtml

Do you want to discover more about the kind of work, the poor working conditions, and the rates of pay in sweatshops? You can also play games at the following site and find out how to help make sure the 2012 Olympics promotes good working conditions for those making official Olympic goods:
http://www.playfair2012.org.uk/game

We are all affected by the global economic crisis, but how can economies recover and avoid so many cuts in public services? Some people think one way is to tax banks and other parts of the financial industry that caused many of the problems. Visit **robinhoodtax.org** to find out more.

The International Museum of Women at has an interesting exhibition, called Economica, that focuses on Women and the Global Economy. The section on microenterprise has accounts from women on how lending has changed their lives. Visit their site:
www.imow.org

You can view a series of informative videos titled "Inside the Global Economy" that covers issues such as protectionism, multinationals, the environment, and development at the following site:
www.learner.org/resources/series86.html

There are many museums and also websites about the slave trade and its importance to the economic development of different cities and countries. Explore the following sites:
www.liverpoolmuseums.org.uk/ism/slavery
www.antislavery.org

View a fascinating and informative four-minute film, made by Hans Rosling, that tells the story of 200 countries over 200 years, revealing how the populations' wealth and life expectancy changed over time:
www.bbc.co.uk/programmes/p00cgkfk

INDEX